The Sound of Water

poems by

Jim Garrett

Finishing Line Press
Georgetown, Kentucky

The Sound of Water

in memory of my father

Copyright © 2018 by Jim Garrett
ISBN 978-1-63534-564-3 First Edition
All rights reserved under International and Pan-American Copyright Conventions.
No part of this book may be reproduced in any manner whatsoever without written permission from the publisher, except in the case of brief quotations embodied in critical articles and reviews.

ACKNOWLEDGMENTS

"In the Batting Cages, Asbury Park, New Jersey, August 16, 1958" first appeared in *Aethlon: The Journal of Sports Literature*
"Opening Day at Ray Chapman's Grave" first appeared in *Spitball: The Literary Baseball Magazine*

Publisher: Leah Maines
Editor: Christen Kincaid
Cover Art and Design: Enrique de la Mata
Author Photo: Michael Starinsky

Printed in the USA on acid-free paper.
Order online: www.finishinglinepress.com
also available on amazon.com

Author inquiries and mail orders:
Finishing Line Press
P. O. Box 1626
Georgetown, Kentucky 40324
U. S. A.

Table of Contents

at the corner of ocean and beach 1
In the Batting Cages, Asbury Park, New Jersey,
    August 16, 1958 2
Season of Light 3
Enough Beach, Enough Time 4
Turtle-Hunting 5
The Sound of Water 6
Sandcastle 8
The Surprising Signs of Drowning 9
Speed Limits 10
A Summer Elegy 12
Four Tides 13
Surfcaster 15
Snow at the Beach 18
Leaving Lookout 19
Learning to Swim at 56 20
The Sea Urchin 22
The Years, Uncounted 23
Driving to the Jersey Shore from Anywhere, U.S.A. 24
Doan Brook 25
The Cure 26
Thousands of Sunsets 28
A History of Turtles 29
Wings 31
Opening Day at Ray Chapman's Grave 32

at the corner of ocean and beach

growing
up
at
the
corner
of
ocean
and
beach
we
taste
salt
air
in
dreams
ever
since

In the Batting Cages, Asbury Park, New Jersey, August 16, 1958

In the batting cages in Asbury Park, New Jersey
Ten months before I was born

I see my father beaming under a bright moon
Throttling a thick bat

I see him glowing in the glare of a spotlight
Crouching, choking up

I see him buffeted by boardwalk breeze
Glowering at the pitching gun

Raising his hands like a god or Willie Mays
He doesn't steal a glance at the walls of Convention Hall

Ripping hard practice cuts
He doesn't hear the carousel's calliope music

Staring down the spinning ball
He doesn't turn his head to the turning Ferris wheel

Striding into the pitch
He doesn't see Tillie's smiling face at Palace Amusements

I see him as crowds move in and out of boardwalk arcades
Slugging liners

I see him as families queue at the Paramount, Walter Reade, and St. James
Swinging for the fences

I see his carousel, Ferris wheel, Palace Amusement, boardwalk arcade
Getting his ups

While my patient mother-to-be on her wedding day
Counts pitches to herself, runs, hits, and errors.

Season of Light

In opening ceremonies of light
across the front porch floor

I find my name in the line-up
my place in the batting order

but after the sun kicks and delivers
its blazing fastball

who knows the score
or the way the game is played

plays deep enough
for a backhand stop

shifts far enough
for a hard liner

lines up close enough
for a corner triple

for the inevitable scorekeeper
the scorecard's always wrong

no fourth strike
no extra inning

the game is played by losing
you win by losing

and it's a game without rules
(as far as I know)

without chance of victory
except for sunlight

Enough Beach, Enough Time

I can't forget those shore summer days
Before I knew anything but time

Always enough beach, enough time
Roaming from Avalon to Stone Harbor

My father piloting us, no compass or sextant,
A path as meandering as a horseshoe crab's

My pouty sister regaled atop his shoulders
Her small hand shading her eyes like a salute

My intrepid sister foraging sand
Her palms filling with bits of treasure

My mother, children's hands in hers, in step
And me, moping alone in the middle of the family,

Empty-handed, eyes canvassing the shore
For places and meanings

In tide's uprush and backwash
Sand's cusps and scarps

A claw in a bed of blue mussels
A whelk shrouded in seaweed

Without knowing what I was looking for
Blinking in the light of that I am

Turtle-Hunting

I used to ask my father to drive slower
Down the coastal road, cross slower
Over the low bridge, go slower down the bay street
Turn slower into the beach lot
Slow enough for me, eight years old,
Face against glass, to look for turtles.

He apologized for going the speed limit
When he had somewhere else to be
But when he didn't, he drove on the berm
Slower than a school bus or mail truck
Warning lights flashing, eyes in rearview
Foot ready to brake for every turtle.

How many times did he drive those same roads
With his son in the backseat dreaming of turtles?
What must it have been like for him, a man
Who sped through life, careering into trouble,
Who took the high road in the fast lane,
To drive so slowly down his son's wonted paths?

The Sound of Water

> "If you cause your ship to stop and place
> the head of a long tube in the water
> and place the outer extremity to your ear,
> you will hear ships at a great distance from you."
> – Leonardo da Vinci, 1490

When I had nothing else to do
summer afternoons at Avalon
instead of running, splashing

or shouting like boys my age
I waded out in the surf alone
put my head underwater

for as long as I could, imagining
I heard unheard sounds
like a short-wave radio

as close to my ear as whispers
too far way to be heard in air
or by anyone not listening

a slurp of a shore I couldn't see
a whoosh of a dropped anchor
a clanging ship at a great distance

a bark of a prowling shark
tintinnabulations of dolphins
a soft hum of a deeper sense

until some boy my age, or my sister,
or a frantic, long-bodied lifeguard
pulled me back, clutching me,

looking long into my eyes, saying
in a pitched voice I couldn't make out
didn't you hear me calling?

why was your head underwater?

Sandcastle

Like a flash of lightning or gust of wind
The wave we expected all afternoon
Working on spec, against odds and deadlines,
Digging trenches, lugging pails, packing walls

Swept away everything before we knew it
Serpentine moat, beach grass bulwarks
Sand-dribbled rococo arches and turrets
Seaweed-enforced labyrinthine walls

Until the castle we built, architects of sand,
Castle of our imagined lives as kings
We left behind without a backward glance
For other boys, beach archeologists, to find

As if childhood afternoons prepared us
For rising tides, rogue waves, storm surges
As if even as boys we knew what was ahead:
Flood damage, power outages, property losses

FOR SALE sign or wrecking ball
Tsunami of pain, rush of an ambulance
Missed good-byes, the end of the make-believe
Whenever we had to leave the beach for home.

The Surprising Signs of Drowning

Hollywood is wrong, the article says,
It doesn't look like it does in the movies.

No splashing, no yelling, no thrashing,
No waving arms, no calling for help

No distress, no panic, no noise. It's quieter.
It's easily unobserved, the experts say,

Body upright in water, arms spread,
Sinking and rising, mouth gaping

Because of "instinctive drowning response"
No waving or calling for help

A silent struggle, not violent or noisy,
Not longer than a minute before

In the last gasp, I imagine, all falls away
As sounds of children fade when rain comes

Speed Limits

We didn't think of speed limits
the summer we fell in love with
driving cars we didn't own
headlights high, windows rolled
speeding where we didn't know
going, going, going, just going
racing every car ahead of us
fleeing every car behind us
the radio dial spinning songs
telling us what to do
urging us where to go
under a tide of sky with stars
like seashells washed up
no map for blind turns
or sudden dead ends
rolling down dark highways
searching for neons of seaside bars
holding onto a promise
of something real happening
on the front lines of growing up
not yet eighteen, armed
with IDs, beer money, and a pledge
to stay wide awake, even all night
like scared soldiers on patrol
looking up and down the shore
in the heat of a summer night
for anyone to know or meet
a fallen angel at the end of a bar
a heavenly song on a jukebox
a beached messiah calling us
any message in any bottle
looking everywhere for everybody

stopping nowhere for nobody
before spraying gravel in bar lots
promising strangers we'll meet again
bellowing broken Bruce lyrics
hurtled from houses into the dark
of a never-ending Jersey night.

A Summer Elegy

for V. K. B. (1957-1980)

When the phone call came, I was in a bathing suit
With my beach towel, beach chair, paperback.
When the phone call came, I was summer at the Jersey shore.

After college exams you wanted to hike the White Mountains.
I wanted to swim the Jersey shore.
When the phone call came, I was summer at the Jersey shore.

No one I know would have loved it as much as you.
I'm telling you again and again how much you would have loved it.
When the phone call came, it was summer at the Jersey shore.

Four Tides

1. Spring Tide at Sandy Hook

Begin at morning light
Go on till late at night

Start at curve of bay
Still more at rocky shore

Behind footprints at first
Ahead of steps at last

At outset, with simple faith,
Keep on, as we do, in doubt

Summoned by shadow's length
    Before cold rain

2. Riptide at Sea Bright

End of first day of summer
Beginning of summer's last

From across the way or upstate
A thousand miles or decade

Alone when with someone
With someone when alone

Out the door across the street
Through the lot up the steps

On the boardwalk over the dunes
    Before the gale

3. Slack Tide at Long Branch

Carriage ride, railroad stop
Fleet of rooms at the Casino

Ladies' fineries, parasols
Boardwalk promenades

Socialites at the Sanford White
A summer place for Presidents

Cottages above the strand
Tents for picnicking

Bloomers and bathing machines
    Before the surge

4. Ebb Tide at Ocean Grove

A beach walk begins
In particular time: dusk, mist, June

Gusts, high tide, Fourth of July
Ninety-eight in shade, August, noon

Begins in particular place: private road
A winding path through dunes

Tall beach grass, an old boat ramp
SWIM AT YOUR OWN RISK

And particular life: still life
    Before landfall

Surfcaster

Walking away down sandy shore
Between high-rise and low tide

I don't see anybody anywhere
This breezeless morning in May

Except construction workers
Preparing condos for summer

No couples astride the drift line
Or busy children digging sand

Nobody toeing the cold tide
Or dreaming in a beach chair

It's too early in the season
To be here this Monday morning

Until beyond pavilion and jetty
I spot a lone surfcaster

In mist and spray
At vigil in surf

Gaze and line unreeling
For a tug to lift him up

A catch, a haul, a prize
From the deep and the dark

And I know why I walk this beach
Why I write these poems

I, surfcaster too, troll the shore
For the tug that lifts me up

A catch, a tie, a connection
Hooked at the end of my line

I cast my eyes around
Widening the net of my gaze

Sandpipers race ahead of me
Seagulls scout my route

Waking from a dream
I don't walk the beach alone

I walk with the tide
Ready to plunge and see

But memories tangle with regrets
Like beach glass in kelp

The past's wrack, silent companion,
Catches up, keeps stride

Tromps along, wends with me
Around jetties, stooping

For shells but finding
What the shore stores up:

Doubts riding waves
Seahorses curled in mid-race

Fears floating on currents
Skeletons of ghost crabs

Waves behind me erasing
My footprints' scrawl

And I'm alone again, nothing
To add to surf's hieroglyph

When I look back
The surfcaster is gone

Snow at the Beach

It snows all night the last night
I stay at the beach house
Not sleeping, watching the traffic light
At the corner of Ocean and Beach
Change color in the falling snow

A floor below, my father
In the hum of a hospital bed
Sighs and gasps sighs and gasps
Again and I wait and again
Until only low labored breaths

Shudder through the old house
No sound of wind or waves
As if snow falling all night
Stops the ceaseless tide
Shore as silent as held breath

And I remember a bitter winter night
When I followed him onto the beach
To hunt the sand for driftwood
And lost sight of him in the dark
My calls drowned in the sound of surf

Leaving Lookout

Big leaky old ship's up for sale
Even captain's left the bridge

I'm not ready to leave lookout
Step down from crow's nest life

Turn away from long-held watch
Let go of ship duty appointed me

When a boy at a high window
Shipshape day before the mast.

From my haunt above swells
I follow captain's orders still

Inspect horizons, fore and aft,
Spy squalls and shoals, close by,

Heed keenings, not far off,
Breathless for news of tidalwaves.

Our ship lists hard now
Unrighted by storm and age

Keel fractured, hull flooded
Ailing captain kept below

Masts unrigged, sails flayed.
Still I keep watch, looking out

For shrouds of dark clouds
Roiling sea, another surge

Before big leaky old ship, home,
Slips off into watery memory.

Learning to Swim at 56

My glasses folded on my towel
Beside the pool at the college

I can't tell what I see or why
I'm taking swimming lessons

Or why I think I'll change my life
Swimming the length of a pool

Or why I never learned to swim
A boy clinging to a pool ladder

Treading water, dog paddling
Wading only to my knees in surf

Watching other boys riding waves
My father plunging headlong

Or why, now at 56, it matters to me
To make it from one end to the other

Without panicking, without stopping
Without gulping or gasping

Because all my life I've stopped
Pulled up, begged off, kept mum

Stayed too long in the shallow end
Content to watch others swim

Too unsure, unwilling, unable
To plunge, kick, and breathe

Find a steady pace, keep calm
Make it to the opposite wall.

When my undergraduate instructor says
Swimming is between you and you

This isn't between you and the pool
Water isn't for you or against you

I try again but stop halfway
Doubts surrounding me

Fears swimming up at me
My finish line still far away.

When he says I have to change
Belief before I can swim

I think of Talmud instructing parents
Teach Torah, trade, and swimming

As if letting go of ladders
Plunging without panicking

Staying afloat in deep waters
Matters as much as God and job

As if moving through water
Buoyed by my own strokes

Or paddling from surf to breaker
Without fear of making it back

Can save me from my drowning
Before I reach the other end.

The Sea Urchin

> "American and coalition forces are in the early stages
> of military operations to disarm Iraq, to free its people
> and to defend the world from grave danger."
> – President George W. Bush, March 21, 2003

That spring break when we traveled where we'd never been
Between fields of first flight and dunes of wild horses

Bombings on TV sounded like waves crashing on the shore
As Baghdad's night sky burst into fireworks on Fourth of July.

In the owners' guestbook I started my entry extolling
Wafts of light and easy surf, soft bed and breezy porch

A walk along Orville's seconds aloft, a glimpse at Corolla
A cup of she-crab soup to die for, my peace in a time of war

But ended writing this question to readers on vacation:
Who can forget the shock and awe of fading light by the seashore?

The Years, Uncounted

All these years I've been counting the years
(what they write in self-help books we shouldn't do)

as if keeping track of dates, marking calendars
saving birthday cards, old IDs, passports

rubber-banding letters, postcards, Mass cards
filing away pay stubs, receipts, tax returns

filling up notebooks, keeping diaries, writing poems
makes them—by accumulation alone—valuable

my thirty-five years this, our twenty-nine years that
his twenty-one years since, her eighteen years before

as if by counting the years I'm counting their worth
—as if time were, in fact, money, which it isn't—

as if it's mathematical—counting years equals a sum
of significance—as if counting confers meaning—

—as we do for a pitcher's career or a queen's reign
or a president's legacy or a CEO's largesse—

as if any number of years—one or forty—changes
how I felt when I looked for you in a crowd

on a Fourth of July night beside the ocean
and found you, and stood beside you, breath held,

and saw you beam under a sky lit by fireworks
a moment lasting until now, a moment incalculable.

Driving to the Jersey Shore from Anywhere, USA

It don't matter what road you're on
Highway 9, Route 88, or 57th Street
Tenth Avenue, Thunder Road, or E Street
If you're driving to the Jersey shore…

It don't matter what car you drive
A '69 Chevy with a 396, a hemi with four on the floor
A pink Cadillac, used car, borrowed car, or stolen car
If you're driving to the Jersey shore…

It don't matter who you're driving with
Terry or Eddie, Bobby, Billy, or Wayne
Wendy or Candy, Rosy or Bobby Jean
If you're driving to the Jersey shore…

It don't matter where you're from
Utah desert, Darlington, or Mahwah
Lincoln, Nebraska, or streets of Philadelphia
If you're driving to the Jersey shore…

It don't matter what you leave behind
Car wash, auto plant, construction job
Daddy's garage, the ties that bind
If you're driving to the Jersey shore…

It don't matter what you hope to find
A reason to believe, a runaway American dream
The promised land, a land of hopes and dreams
If you're driving to the Jersey shore…

Take the backstreets. Drive all night.

Doan Brook

> "Doan Brook is a seven-mile stream feeding from
> Shaker Lakes that crosses Euclid Avenue and runs
> through Wade Park before emptying into Lake Erie."
> – Encyclopedia of Cleveland History

A June night, after long cool rain,
I wait up listening for something
Not cars splashing through puddles
Or water pouring from downspouts.
It seems lighter at night after rain.

I wait up listening for something
Not engines, horns, alarms, sirens
Or warbles, growls, screeches, moans
Not even the faint rumble of trains
Out of the old Collinwood railyard.

I wait up listening for something
A hum, a brush of water on stone
A faint gurgle beneath the ground
Not rain water seeping in gutters
Or storm sewers banking surges.

I wait up listening for something
Like the sound of water dripping
On a petal of a rose after a storm
Or the whisper we hear beneath
The rushing waves of our lives.

I wait up listening for something
Submerged, tunneled, echoed
A murmur we all hear within.
I wait up listening for something
In the silence of Doan Brook.

The Cure

> *"The cure for anything is salt water: sweat, tears or the sea."*
> – Isak Dinesen

Bug bite, skinned knee, stubbed toe
Cut finger, scraped elbow, bruised shin

My mother told me: put salt water on it
You'll feel better before you know it

Sunburned, thirsty, out of breath
Hungry, tired, too long in the sun

Left behind on the playground
Embarrassed, afraid of the ball

My mother told me: run around a bit
You'll feel better before you know it

First day at new school, lost in the halls
Missing homework, teacher's call

Called third strike, cut from the team
Missed free throw, left on the bench

My mother told me: take a dip
You'll feel better before you know it

Speeding ticket, fender bender
Too much, too long at closing time

Home too early or too late from a date
Unable or unwilling to alibi

At the top of the stairs, leaving home,
Afraid to step away, be on my own

My mother told me: go ahead, let it out,
You'll feel better before you know it

Walking from a friend's funeral in the heat
After kneeling and saying good-bye

I don't need my mother to tell me
Why I taste the seashore on my lips

Thousands of Sunsets

I've seen thousands of sunsets
I've forgotten, didn't notice.

Some I noticed but didn't see.
Some sunsets bothered me.

Others blinded my drive home.
Some satisfied me, day ended.

Most I ignored. Something else
Mattered more than the sunset.

A few I watched absently
So lost in thought about me.

Yet on a footbridge over a dam
After a long walk in cool May

As a great blue heron rises
Like a ghost in a cathedral

A sunset at Horseshoe Lake
No different from others

Blinks on and off like stars
Into thousands of sunsets.

A History of Turtles

After I saw the turtle in the grass close to the road
I went on walking around the lake as if I could go on

And not go back. I was alone, listening to a podcast
On poetry. I'm fifty-seven years old. I took a nap

Before I left for my walk. I knew breeds of turtles
When I was a boy. I used to jog around this lake.

The podcast was about a Seamus Heaney poem
About his attic. I wore sunglasses. My knees hurt.

I haven't seen or looked for a turtle since I was ten
When I carried around the T book of *World Book*.

I walked on, thinking about thinking about
How far I would go before (or if) I turned back.

I don't make decisions. I think about them a lot.
I wrote a poem about when I hunted for turtles

From the backseat of my father's car but the poem
Isn't really about turtles. It's about my father's life.

After we looked for turtles, my father brought me
A turtle—a terrapin—home from Florida that died.

I used to keep baby turtles from the pet store.
What if I don't go back to see what happened?

Because once, fifty years ago, I found a baby turtle
In seaweed. I looked for seahorses and starfish, too.

I could have gone on walking and I did go on
Since I still had a half a mile to go before I –

My son and my father are too far away from me.
If I could go back, I could find why I am alone

Walking around a lake, thinking about turtles.
I went back. I didn't see the turtle at first.

I didn't want to look for my mistake in the road.
It turned out I wasn't looking in the right place.

When I picked him up, he closed up but not all the way.
I have recently been closed up but not all the way.

I hurried to put him back down, away from the road,
In tall grass that led down through trees to the lake.

I don't know why I hurried to put him down.
I wanted to take him home and start over again.

My son kept a turtle named Joe in his bedroom.
I waited to see him disappear in the underbrush

But my turtle didn't move the way turtles don't.
Sons move away from fathers, sometimes slowly

Sometimes fast. I left my turtle behind, hoping
He'd slip away *towards* the water not the road

But when I looked back, I couldn't see my turtle
My red-eared slider, my diamondback terrapin

My long-necked snapper, my Galapagos tortoise
My grown boy, my aged dad, even my self

And couldn't tell where he was or which way
He went, leaving me alone listening to poetry.

Wings

> Tinton Falls, New Jersey
> October 29, 2012

At the hospital on Hope Road
news flashes evacuate

lights stay on
wheelchairs whine

orderlies change
bedsheets

nurses check
monitors

patients sleep
my father waits for wings

IVs drips
bedpans fill

out of the flood
my mother appears

he says ... turn around
show them your wings

Opening Day at Ray Chapman's Grave

Lake View Cemetery, Cleveland, Ohio

Opening Day, I'm up, leave my dugout life
Cross at the light and enter through the gate
With Cleveland cap, souvenir Louisville Slugger,
And scuffed baseball I could have pitched
To my son in the park just a few years ago
Or my father could have pitched to me
Forty years ago when I stood in, afraid of
The ball, his sidearm delivery, a beanball.

Inside the stadium of Lake View Cemetery
Spring frost still clinging to headstone rows
I hurry past Garfield's grand monument
And pay no attention to Rockefeller's obelisk
Instead I imagine a grounds crew at work
Tending grass around Ray Chapman's stone
And a crowd arriving for Opening Day
With bats, balls, and gloves as tributes.

Closer, I imagine a gathering, infielders at the mound,
Mickey Cochran, Tony Conigliaro, Dickie Thon,
Kirby Puckett, even Charles "Cupid" Pinckney,
Class "B" infielder for the Dayton Veterans in 1909,
His grave only a short walk (if only!) from Chapman's,
Who in the dusk of a seventh inning didn't see
Or couldn't dodge a fatal 3-0 pitch, a beanball

That struck behind his left ear, and I wouldn't be surprised
If every one of them swore he'd give up anything,
Even eternal rest, for one more chance at the plate,
As I would, to stand in again, my ailing father pitching again.

Jim Garrett has taught literature and writing in the English Department at University School, an independent boys' school outside of Cleveland, Ohio, for the past thirty-five years. A graduate of Oberlin College and Cleveland State University, he is the author of two earlier poetry chapbooks *At the Five-and-Dime, Lavallette, New Jersey* (Finishing Line Press, 2007) and *Innkeepers of Shorelight* (Finishing Line Press, 2011) and has published poems in *The Plum Creek Review, The Record, The Carroll Quarterly, The Lyric, The Listening Eye, Journal of New Jersey Poets, Exit 13, The Penwood Review, Aethlon: Journal of Sports Literature,* and *Spitball: The Literary Baseball Magazine.* A father of an adult son and a grandfather of a brand-new grandson, he and his wife Margaret live in Cleveland Heights, Ohio, but he returns to the Jersey shore every summer to collect poems on the beach.

www.ingramcontent.com/pod-product-compliance
Lightning Source LLC
LaVergne TN
LVHW041509070426
835507LV00012B/1444